The Answers Are Outside The Building

By Stu Heilsberg

Printed Edition

ISBN 978-0-9882507-2-7

Table of Contents

1

Why This Book?

"I don't know."

Wow.

That's a tough one to say in business. And, in fact, seems to be considered the kiss of death in many situations.

I contest, however, that it is not only acceptable, but liberating, and perhaps the best mindset to have to truly serve my company and my customers. Based on my education and my work experience, many either think or expect that I should know a lot or have a lot of answers.

But I learn much more and do much more for others *by admitting what I don't know and getting to the best external resources.*

What I am going to do in this book is share my experience with embracing this concept of "not knowing."

It can, and certainly does, assist with many areas of business, but I will focus mostly on business and customer development; I have experiences at Intuit and Qualcomm that I will share. I have also been the CEO of a startup, so the ideas and approaches I am recommending have been proven in businesses of all sizes and across several industries.

I'm passionate about this concept and approach. Very passionate. The reason is simple: I want to do things that are truly useful, and I want to be of service. I've learned that the best, and sometimes only, way to learn what these things are is to ask people. That's it. I have to ask them. I cannot figure it out on my own, and I cannot figure it out in a vacuum.

But when we get together in conference rooms and put our best opinions and guesses on the table in an effort to conclude, that's what we are doing. We're creating the best logical hypotheses we can, however, they're not based in fact. I don't think this serves anyone well at all.

This approach really came into its own when I worked on researching and launching three new businesses for Qualcomm. Each was separate and mostly unrelated to Qualcomm's semiconductor and licensing businesses, so they were quite autonomous.

I often describe them as "like startups, without the fear of missing payroll." I think walking through this period in my career will be useful context for the rest of this book.

When I joined Qualcomm I had never done business development as a formal and specifically titled role before. There were about four of us in the business group on my first project. It was a big effort, highly visible, and estimated to be a billion dollar business for Qualcomm if brought to fruition.

I was asked to engage, get to know, and formulate a business strategy for my assigned section of the ecosystem. So I went on the road, and got to know the companies I was assigned to. I met them, got to know what was important to them, and identified with their help a bunch of other companies I should get to know.

So I got on more airplanes, and got to know those other companies, too. I traveled about 40% of the time, including internationally, and loved it. Not so much because of the logistics of traveling, but because I came back smarter after every trip. *I showed up with real, indisputable feedback from prospective partners and customers that no one else had.*

Something else very, very important was happening. I was creating a checklist of all those members of the ecosystem that I could learn from. Not just those at we might sell to, but anyone that I could teach me how to define a product and sell better.

And finally, I was starting to prioritize a pipeline.

We were a big company, so we wanted and thought we needed big, marquee names to prove to ourselves and the market that our solution was validated and worthy.

But guess what? The big guys take a long time to decide and take action. One of my lead investors at a startup I led burned in to my brain the phrase "18 months to close a big company."

I have yet to prove him wrong.

So while I engaged and worked really hard on those big guys, I also worked in parallel to build a pipeline of ecosystem members that would take action sooner, validate our solution well, and start the revenue steam quickly. This concept of a second, more practical pipeline was not taught at any company I worked for (the absence of one is usually preferred, actually). I learned this from leading that startup.

So over a number of months we gathered feedback from all over the ecosystem and the world. We put it together, defined a roadmap that was consistent with the needs of the market and the business priorities of the ecosystem. Now we needed to get some deals done. Some for partnerships, and some for customers and revenue.

Guess what? We already knew who they all were! We knew which companies wanted our solution and which ones we wanted to work with first. And because of our approach we had built *relationships*, not sales leads. The former being much more valuable to my company.

And so a few quarters passed. We signed up the right ecosystem members and started to put it all together, based on what we had learned. Qualcomm then acquired a key member of the ecosystem for an enormous amount of money and set up an entire division to build the business.

The second project comes along, and I'm asked to lead the entire business side of the effort. We had a technology looking for a home. Classic. Good stuff, though, and appeared to be able to solve real pain for end users. I just needed to find out what pain that was and how to make the most money from it.

So I just did it again. I created a simple ecosystem outline, engaged members in each area, listened to what they said was and wasn't important, outlined the top opportunities, and reported back to Qualcomm with a plan. Worked like a charm. We had a very good feel for the top two use cases to address, the key players needed to execute, and a strong outline of the value chain and where we sat. The business was green-lighted, and a division was set up.

On to the third project. By this time, something really started to click. The short version was "get an engagement list together, and leave the building." So I did. Right out of the gate I defined success as not spending all five days in the office in any given week. If I did, then I wasn't moving things along fast enough.

The result was the same as projects one and two, only I got there much faster and with even better definition and guidance on what to do. I had meaningful engagements with sixty companies in just forty-five days. I was on fire. The industry was one that I had never been in before, but within that short time I had become the expert. All I did was go spend time with the right folks and listen really well!

I have always respected, appreciated, and gravitated towards being customer-focused first, and technology-driven second. The phase of my career that I just shared allowed me to put that into action at a business development and P&L level like never before.

As you move through this book you'll see a number of suggestions for processes and tactics to execute on those processes. Learn from them, and use them, but don't lose sight of why they exist.

We are looking to drive P&L growth, I will admit, but that's the measure of success. We achieve that success, though, by doing truly useful things and by being of service. If the things we do in business don't measure up on these two fronts, then we won't sell anything. Period.

So to do this we need to learn the mindsets, attitudes, willingness, and listening skills needed to serve our customers and employers well. It is these things that are so often overlooked, but ironically they are the keys to executing processes well and getting the desired results. Be sure to keep in mind that it all comes back to the idea that embracing "I don't know" is a good thing.

A very good thing.

So I've written this book, because I've shared this approach with several respected colleagues, and they seem to consistently take out a pen and begin to take notes. They state that they love the idea, but very few seem to do it this way. I finally came to the conclusion that if people I greatly respect think enough of this approach to take actual notes, perhaps I should share it with a broader audience to be of service.

That's my hope here - that you find some insight and value from this book that can in some way be of service to you. And perhaps you'll pass on a bit to others.

2

"I Don't Know" is a Good Thing

So I think my whole life I've been taught to make sure I have the answer.

In grade school my task was to study and do well on tests. In undergraduate and graduate school things advanced a bit to a goal of working with others to "figure out the right approach and answer" as a team.

In the early years of my career I was allowed to be a bit ignorant, but was warned (sometimes literally and sometimes by seeing the scolding of others) that I better have some answers. Then, as my responsibilities elevated, got broad across business(es), and I became an executive it got really hard. Then I needed to have answers to "whatever question might come up when we meet with the big boss."

I don't think this served me, my employers, my partners, or my customers well. The focus was on having the answers instead of doing useful things and being of service.

You know, it's funny.

My dad used to say "If all else fails, follow the directions." It was funny and cute, but it was also a good reminder that when it's getting difficult you should fall back on the basics. Somewhere along the way I adapted this phrase to an approach in business; When things start to get complicated on how I message or speak to folks, because I'm not sure how to spin or pitch or explain something, I try to remember to say "If all else fails, tell the truth."

This has served me well, especially when I simply don't know something. Just admit it. Really. Admit it, focus on some solid approaches to get the answers from those that have them, and move fast on getting those answers.

Okay, so that last sentence was the big idea.

Yup. And most when they read it or hear it agree wholeheartedly. They even try to do it more. They are already doing it to some degree. But the point is to make it a *fundamental approach*. What I mean is that it's not just one of the tactics to figure out a good business plan or channel strategy. It *is* the approach. To not truly make it part of your DNA means that it will likely not be done enough, will be difficult to execute, and most importantly will not stick.

So now it's time to dissect the title of this book: "The answers are outside the building." I spent a fair amount of time figuring out what I wanted to say with the title, and I have several key points rolled into that title that outline the big idea I want to share. I'll take each one-by-one:

The Answers

Clearly this is a very broad comment, but typically my experience has been that "the answers" relates to what people want.

What do they want to buy? How much they will pay for it?

Where they will go to get it? What they will do with their old solution? What competition might they look at? What will the competition do or not do?

Will they adopt those "new technologies" that might compete with our product? What does my distribution channel want and not want? Would a new distribution channel work better? Will the channel take inventory fast?

Will that key partner sign the deal to work with us soon? Will those customers buy now? And many more questions.

Most would agree that is a reasonable list of questions for starting, running, or optimizing a business. Many would agree that the real list is much longer. Either way, the point is these answers mostly relate to what *other* members of the ecosystem want.

Not us. Not me. Not my company. If I want the answers to these questions, I need to go get them from *others*.

So think broadly here. Be open to *any* question and answer combination that applies. Even the simple ones. It's critical that we get accurate info, and even those "obvious" answers can be wrong if we are using our opinion or best guesses to fill in the blanks. Commit to this, and you and your company will get much smarter. These answers are what tell you how to do truly useful things and to be of service.

Are Outside

Okay, so we've got our questions. Good. Great stuff. Fantastic.

Now... Stop!

Do *not* try to answer them.

We just agreed (I hope) that *they* have the answers. This is hard, though, as a natural inclination is to "figure it out". Sometimes we justify analyses on these questions by saying "Well, for me to be properly prepared, I need to have a proposal or a pitch."

I'll speak much, much more about this later, but for now let's just say that's a misleading justification that will slow us down, bias us, and most importantly not serve our customers or companies very well.

We are and typically work with bright people, so it's natural to think we should be able to come up with the answers, right? Well, maybe some good logical hypotheses, yes. But the answers? Not usually.

There's too much info, context, perspective, and more in the hands and minds of our ecosystem partners for us to have the whole picture. So let's leverage them to help us here. And maybe go a step further by embracing the idea that my best guesses may only be close and will usually be wrong.

Perhaps we should even default to not even trying to answer the questions in an attempt to remain open and listen well?

The Building

"Building" does not refer just to the office or place that we sit. It includes that, but the building is my office, my car, my computer, my presentations, and perhaps most importantly my mind.

The key point here is that the answers are not usually within my company or within me. I need to go elsewhere to get them. This point is akin to the "Outside" section above, but it helps to remind us of the places we can easily slip into trying to figure it out ourselves.

Just because we didn't hold a meeting to formulate answers doesn't mean that we might not try to figure it out as we are preparing some slides or discussing it over lunch with a colleague. Again... Stop. Not in "the Building."

That covers the first part of the Big Idea and our title. But I had a second sentence to the title at one point that read "Embrace it." I didn't think a two-sentence title made a whole lot of sense, so I dropped, it. However, it's a critical part of the message, so I'd like to dissect it also.

Embrace

We're going to get a little intangible, but it's important. This word has served me well, and made this process more effective, as well as more fun.

One definition of embrace is "to accept or support (a belief, theory, or change) willingly and enthusiastically."

Yikes! That sounds like I need to do things very differently. If it sounds like that to you then you're getting the point.

This is not just a nice slogan. It's a mindset, an attitude, a philosophy, or maybe even a spirituality. Regardless, it's deep. The word "enthusiastically" says it all.

So by "embrace" I mean *really* accept it. It's easy to say it. It's easy to agree with the logic. I see and hear folks agree with this "outside" approach a lot. But embracing that the answers are outside the building requires an attitude that has the potential to change almost everything we do.

It means I need to put myself second (no matter how smart I think I am.) It means I have to wait to get the answers, which I personally hate, by the way. It means that I don't know everything. And perhaps the hardest to accept is that it means I may need to admit this ignorance to others.

And as I indicated in the Introduction, we're pretty much taught not to do this in business. So this is a tough one to really do. But I encourage you to hear this word, Embrace. It can, and likely will, change the game for you.

It

Small word, big meaning.

"It" is not a business tactic. It's not a strategy. It's not a slogan. It's not small. It's big. It's something that will change the game. It's an attitude that will require work, because it's different.

As we just reviewed in our "Embrace" section, this is not a superficial tactic or slogan to throw around. It's a fundamental mindset and approach that guides all that I do. So the definition of "it" is less important here than the simple (but sometimes tough) realization and acceptance that "it" is big.

Really big.

This approach really is asking you to not just change some of how you do business, but quite possibly to change yourself.

Now that we've grounded ourselves in the subtle, but big, meaning behind the title, let's look a bit at how things are done today.

To do something truly useful and to be of service I need to embrace the concept of "I don't know." For me to learn how to do these things for others I need to admit that they know more about their needs than I.

I've embraced "I Don't Know" with companies hundreds of times, probably thousands. It turns out well every time. Sometimes a bit neutral, but never bad. In fact, an important realization for me has been that my audience members already knew that I didn't know, and for me to show up pretending otherwise would've been foolish.

Imagine that.

We typically work with smart people. Really smart. And what we are inclined to do is try to figure things out ourselves. I've mentioned this before, but we're going to dive into this a bit now, as it not only is the primary "competitor" to going outside the building, but the very nature of it is emotional, and therefore, tough to navigate and change.

To do useful things and be of service we need to understand, truly believe, and admit to ourselves this status quo. And parts of this status quo can serve us all well. I've found, however, that there are many instances when an alternative approach can be of even more service.

We might be smart or we might think we're smart. Neither is bad, and either can serve customers and employers well when implemented responsibly. This leads us quite naturally, though, to formulate hypotheses and answer questions ourselves.

Not really a bad exercise, but it can be a slippery slope if too much time is allocated or we forget that they are *hypotheses*. And when working in technical industries with engineers that really like to solve problems, this is a force to be reckoned with.

Let's take an example, just so we're completely on the same page.

We've got an existing product line selling reasonably well, but we suspect there is room to improve the P&L and our position in the value chain. We guess that moving volume from away from one of our distributors and selling direct to customers in that channel will allow us to get a bigger piece of the pie.

And after all, we have direct relationships with that distributor's customers anyway, so what's the harm?

Sure, the distributor won't be happy, but we will do our best to be polite and part ways as comfortably as possible. And we won't be using them anymore, so if it goes a little south, we should still be okay.

Now, rather than dissect this strategy and the positives and negatives, let's outline what I've typically seen happen in the conference room when a situation like this arises.

It starts with what the distributor might do to cause problems for us. That goes on for a while (sometimes rearing it's ugly head in several meetings.) At some point the idea of our other distributors and what they might think, feel, fear, or do will come up.

We discuss customers and whether or not they'll be okay with this, which will almost assuredly move the discussion into why they will be okay. After all, we'll pass on some of this larger revenue share to them.

Pricing will be brought up and batted around. Will we charge the same as the distributor? More for some additional services we'll bundle in? Less because of the aforementioned reason? And so on.

There is nothing wrong with asking and attempting to answer these questions. It's a healthy and useful exercise. The issue, I suggest, is that we try to *conclude* the answers. And—boy—do we churn to get to that supposed conclusion when we do this inside the building.

Was it Susan Powter that became famous for her infomercial with the catch phrase "Stop the Insanity!"? I'd rather not identify with an infomercial in this book, but perhaps the situation I'm outlining does warrant a phrase akin to that.

So: this is where I start to lose it, quite frankly.

I'm in this meeting - or series of meetings - where we try to answer these questions, over and over. And because there are truly some smart people in the room, some very logical hypotheses are presented. (Note that the terms "logical" and "hypotheses" are very deliberate word choices.) Typically they each have a counter-hypothesis from someone else the room, which only compounds the ping-pong effect.

I don't know about you, but at this point I'm thinking, "C'mon, man, let's just go ask someone."

So somewhere in here the idea may get thrown on the table to talk to a customer or two. But what I typically see happen is almost a violent reaction to not go "until we have our pitch."

Let's take a minute on this one, as it's incredibly important that this be very clear in your minds —*that it hit you really hard right now.*

What I see over and over and over again is an unwillingness, or perhaps a fear, to talk to anyone outside the building until the "sales pitch" is complete.

This is the problem. This is the perfect illustration of what this book suggests you never do. How can we have a good sales pitch that serves the ecosystem well if we haven't talked to them?

This, ladies and gentlemen, is why I am writing this book.

But (huge but) this really is status quo in most places. And perhaps it should be recognized as such and accepted to some healthy degree, if we're going to steer things in a different direction.

I don't mean "go along with it", I mean accept it as a baseline from which we can change. I have spent part of my career frustrated by things at aren't done "the right way", and this is no exception. I've found, though, that I can be of more service if I criticize less and attempt to understand and work *with* people more.

I don't think this fear-of-saying-I-don't-know phenomenon exists because we are foolish. I think it's because of emotional drivers.

I was taught a very important lesson a few years back by a very accomplished businessman, mentor, and friend. He suggested that I learn to identify the difference between "logical" and "emotional".

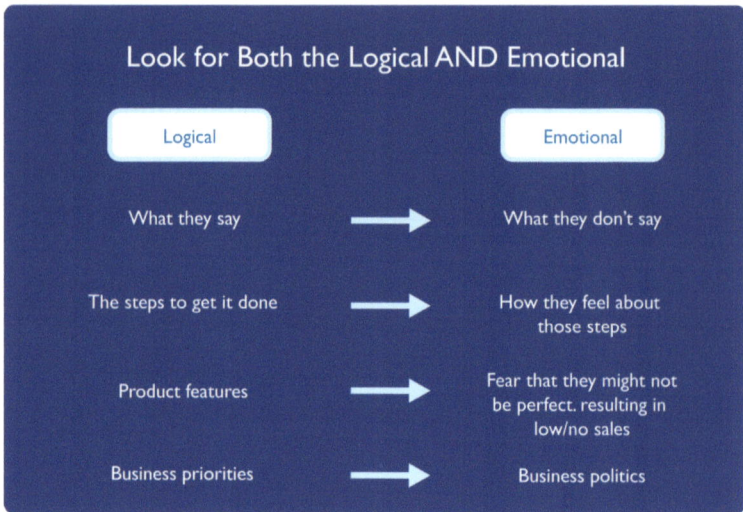

Look for Both the Logical AND Emotional

Logical		Emotional
What they say	→	What they don't say
The steps to get it done	→	How they feel about those steps
Product features	→	Fear that they might not be perfect. resulting in low/no sales
Business priorities	→	Business politics

It came about, because I was frustrated that a group at work was not getting an idea that was incredibly clear to me. And one that I was sure that would help our organization.

I couldn't understand how they were not connecting the dots. It was so clear! Then I learned that there were other factors at play. Some related to perceptions and some driven by factors completely unrelated, but still affecting, my idea. I needed to accept that I had to (first and foremost) learn what these other factors were, be empathetic, and modify my approach in order to be of service to my coworkers.

I was not going to help anyone if I did not fit myself to meet their needs.

Another emotional hot button I've identified is "If we don't give them a pitch, then they may take things down a path that we don't want."

So maybe there's some fear that we're opening ourselves up to something we don't want?

Okay, that's understandable. Who can't relate to that? But maybe by discussing it we can find some positive reasons why even this fear being realized could be acceptable.

Maybe if we do hear a contrarian view from a partner or customer it'll provide us insight on their business priorities. And maybe we wouldn't have heard it or learned about it otherwise.

And if it's a path we don't like, maybe we will simply choose not to go down that path. And if we don't have the option and leverage over that partner or customer to make that choice shouldn't we know about this path as soon as possible?

There are many reasons why this fear does all of us a disservice. Don't let it get in the way.

"I don't know." I started the book with this for a reason.

Fear of "I don't know" is a driving force for this status quo. Perhaps, it's *the* driving force.

It's unnatural to say and admit this. Especially as an executive in charge of building or running a business. It's humbling. It makes us vulnerable. And it might even get us in trouble, depending upon the culture we work in.

Do not underestimate the power of this reluctance to admit ignorance. It might be conscious, but likely is not. It is tricky. Look for it, and don't wait to somehow be informed that this is part of the problem. It's almost always there.

Make this a checkbox in your "What could be happening here?" list.

Or better yet: ask the question "Where was this question answered? Inside the building or outside?"

3

It's About People

Everyone agrees with this. "People are the way you make sales happen", "You've got to have a great network", "It's all about referrals", and so on. But this is not what I'm referring to by this title.

If it were, you'd be able to choose from a plethora of sales networking books already written. What I am referring to here is making people a priority. Make them the focus of your interactions. Make them the source of your guidance. Listen to them. Get to know them and what's important to them in their business. Find out what is truly valuable to them and how you can be of service - literally.

I like to "follow the breadcrumbs" when it comes to people. What I mean by this is each interaction I have with someone gives me a piece of the puzzle I'm trying to solve, and it usually leads me to the next interaction I should have.

There are two things you need to accept when doing this, though. The first is that you are following breadcrumbs, so you need them all before you'll have the final answer and conclusion. So each interaction requires patience, as it is likely only giving me a little of the info I need. It's going to take multiple or many interactions to get to the endpoint.

The second point of acceptance relates to not knowing where things are headed.

When you follow breadcrumbs you are allowing yourself to be led to a location you typically don't know about beforehand. The same goes here. If I don't accept this, then I'll be leading (myself and others!) to a conclusion that I already have formed.

That's the opposite of what we want to do. Remember we are *following* breadcrumbs, not dropping them.

How to Connect

I get my answers from people. I learn from them. Quite frankly, I get my energy from people. If I don't interact with new people enough, I slow down. My goal is to interact with at least two new people each week. And certainly at least one person - new or otherwise - each day.

There are a number of ways I connect with people.

First, I reach out to my favorite people just to touch base and hear how they are. They usually want to know about me, too. Because they are folks that I have excellent synergy with, good things come of these conversations.

This is a group of maybe a dozen or so folks. These are rich relationships that are not tied to or necessarily associated with any specific market or domain. Our connection is mostly based on style, attitude, and sometimes passion for a using a certain skill set.

Also, I've found that I'm given the opportunity to engage with people much more than I ever knew. I get emails from folks offering to have coffee or catch up. There was a time in my career when I thought that it was appropriate to make that happen if that person somehow lined up with an agenda I currently had or if I maybe had the time. I don't do that anymore.

With very, very few exceptions, I have found that people reach out to me for a reason, so when someone reaches out to me my default is a resounding "yes." Can be a call or coffee, and it doesn't need to have an agenda. My best interactions are those that do *not* have an agenda, actually. We simple take turns catching up and let the conversation go where it makes the most sense.

In addition, I am reminded of some of my favorite folks somewhat regularly. But I didn't always act on that in the past either. I was too busy, perhaps. Or maybe I meant to do it, but forgot. But if someone important or relevant from my past somehow comes up via a general email update or online social community, I think that happens for a reason.

They stand out to me, because I've had a good, synergistic connection with them in the past. And why wouldn't that happen again? So I reach out with a quick email offering to catch up over coffee "sometime soon."

They almost always come to fruition, and I almost always end up learning something that helps me with current projects. And, yes, leads or specific business introductions come of those interactions, but I let those things happen on their own time and with almost no direction from me.

There is a common thread in all this.

These people are usually connected to or somehow sent to me by other people that know me well.

That's important. Very important.

There is a natural built-filter because of this, which leads to very rich engagements that are relevant and pre-engaged to some degree. This fundamental approach to connecting with people has served me very well. It's a style and an attitude more than it is a process. If you think of it that way, you'll likely grow to be much better at connecting, connecting for its own sake.

Why to Connect

First, people have the answers. There's an important point in this statement-- "the answers." It's not about finding the decision-makers or getting leads or moving a deal through the pipeline. Those are all things that need to get done, but not in this section.

This section is about getting in front of a lot of people and listening.

Not for me and my objectives, but to understand them and what they need. And the biggest learnings for me many times come in very small messages, small messages that come up over and over again.

So it's not one person that typically gives me the answers, it's the common threads in what I hear across a larger group of conversations. This takes patience, but the learnings are rich and truly useful.

Second, people teach me things. And many, many times they teach me things that I otherwise would not know I needed to learn. This is akin to but very different than my first point. In my first point, I'm looking for answers to questions that I have or might come up with during the process. This is about what *else* I am being told.

Third, people introduce me to other people that can teach me. Not to generate leads, but to teach me. It's important to have this mindset for two reasons. The first is that if I'm focused on getting the lead I don't listen as well. I end up constantly looking for that deliverable and biasing the conversation towards that.

Second, it shows. Meaning that folks know when I am trying to get something for myself. If you focus on the kind of open, agenda-free interactions that I am suggesting in this chapter you will not have to look for the leads.

They will be handed to you. This I promise.

Fourth and final, people are my opportunity to give back, teach, and introduce other great people to each other.

This sounds like the typical "yes, it's good to give back" type of thing, but it can also be a bit selfish, too. Sharing what I learn from others with the people I'm speaking with furthers the dialogue to other great connections. That sharing also confirms what I might be interpreting from others, and I get to use whomever is in front of me as a sounding board.

Also, by introducing great people to other great people, I'm building relationships that will allow me to learn more in the future.

Why This Works

People are a great way to meet other people.

What I mean by this is that we are natural filters for people like us. In addition, people know of other people that might have some synergy with my objectives, so relying on others to steer me to the right people is an extremely useful process.

Note here that I did not say "use people to introduce me other people". I said "relying on others to *steer* me". There's one *very* big difference between these two.

By letting good people steer me to others that can provide me with answers implies that I don't necessarily know the right people to get to. There it is again: "I don't know."

By continuing to embrace this I will be aimed towards folks that I otherwise would never meet. If I have an agenda and closed target list of folks to meet, I'm not going to broaden my horizons. The assumption here is that we surround ourselves with good, smart people that get to know us, and we get to know them.

This is not networking to me. This is connecting with great people.

The goal is not to pitch them. The goal is for them to get to know us. These are completely different engagement models.

Make no mistake. If you have even a hint of sales pitch in your engagement, you will undermine your objective. So you will likely need to go to a bit of an extreme to be sure they know you are not looking for anything from them except some feedback, guidance, and maybe introductions to others that can teach us.

I cannot emphasize enough, ladies and gentlemen, how important people are.

They have the answers or they will guide you to them. They will teach you what you need to know. They will teach you what you need to know even when you didn't know you needed to know it.

And most importantly, people are the reason why we do what we do - We are here to serve them. When we keep this in mind, we not only do a better job and do it with less effort, but we will drive more P&L results. The irony, though, is that those P&L results come when we don't focus on them, but rather focus on people.

4

Do Not Sell

Okay, so this is it.

The big kahuna. The grand idea. The chapter to read if you have no patience and need instant gratification. This is what I've found to be the best way to do useful things and to be of service in business and customer development, and I can confirm that on a very regular basis it continues to prove itself invaluable, pleasantly surprising, and exciting.

Get The Right Mindset

We've spent some time walking through some examples of status quo. And we identified this flawed fundamental approach of "go out after we get a sales pitch."

So the silver bullet is to go out deliberately *without* a sales pitch.

That's it. Don't sell. Yes, I said it. Don't sell. No pitch, no pitch, no pitch!

Now for those of you that are in sales or business development with revenue targets, you probably are ready to close the book. That's okay. This isn't always for you. You need to go close deals and hit the numbers for solutions that are *already* defined.

This is for those in business that need to still define, direct, steer, strategize, and put into action business plans that give you something to sell later. In other words, they still need to identify what is truly useful and how to be of service.

There is a fundamental belief here that the *ecosystem* will dictate to us what it wants, needs, is willing to adopt, and will sell for us.

It is not us and our firm that will dictate these things.

If we try to fight this truth, overlook it, or deliberately ignore it we will fail. So our mission is to go to them to find out what they want, decide if that serves our business well, and then choose to participate or not. This should feel different. It should feel like we are not thinking about ourselves or our companies first.

It should feel like our mission is not to take, but to serve. This is one of those areas that should feel not just like this is a process or strategy change, but perhaps a change in ourselves at almost a personal level.

Just Ask Two Questions of All Ecosystem Members

So how do we "not sell". Simple. After giving a brief and unbiased summary of my firm's concept, I ask two questions of any and every ecosystem member I meet with:

Does this concept fit with your business priorities?

If it does, how can it best serve you?

No slides. No big pitch. No telling them why they need it. Just two questions.

The results are astounding. What I've learned by doing this over and over again is amazing. I get answers not only to the questions I listed while back in the building, but *I get answers to questions I didn't even know I should ask.* And *that* is the lesson of a lifetime.

Now I will admit that the devil is in the details. There are a number of methods I use to set up the concept.

And there are really a whole bunch of objectives hidden in those two questions I listed here. So let's look at what's behind all of this.

The Setup

I mentioned rather casually to give a summary of my firm's concept. But isn't that a sales pitch? It could be, but if you're open to what I'm suggesting in this book, you'll embrace with every fiber of your being some way to *not* make it a sales pitch. And you'll have to find your own way on this, so that it fits your style.

The method that works best for me is to come up with a verbal elevator pitch. Verbal to ensure that I don't make a visit to the town of slideville and start to say too much. Don't get me wrong, I love slides.

But not here. I might in a few sentences say what my company is "thinking of doing" and "that I'm talking to a few members of the ecosystem like them to get their feedback."

Let's take a minute to talk about that last sentence. It's important. First, we are "thinking of doing it", because we're not sure yet. We don't know if anyone wants it. We may not have even started.

And, in fact, let's send the message that it's not done yet, so that "you couldn't even buy it now if you wanted to." *All points aimed at staying out of sales mode.*

The second quote, "talking to other members of the ecosystem like them to get their feedback" has a number of hidden points.

First, we're engaging the *entire* ecosystem. We're not just talking to one section of the value chain. Second, we're talking to other companies like yours - your competitors - so you might want to engage with me a little on this.

If it's a good idea, one of the other ecosystem members might jump and beat them to it. While this might appear threatening, the intent is to be of service to them by nudging them if they are on the fence.

And lastly, we are getting "feedback", not collecting purchase orders. Just talking, folks. Just talking.

And sometimes the initial contact needs to be done via email.

No worries. This approach and content works exactly the same way. Use the same concise words, and use them in the same order. Don't be afraid to have an intro email that is three-to-five sentences. In fact, strive for it.

I'll be realistic and admit that some people do want a pitch. It's been a vast minority from my experience, but it's happened. Most, though, filter themselves out during the meeting setup process, so let's cover that a bit now.

The key here is to avoid getting ourselves, or our audience members, set up with expectations of a sales pitch.

They're used to this, so we need to pull them out of that vortex and work hard to make sure we succeed at this. I have found that using phrases like "I'll be in your area on x day, and I was wondering if I could stop by for a few minutes" or "Do you have 30 minutes to get acquainted and see if there might be some synergies between our organizations?" Lots of words intended to keep it casual and set expectations of a *dialogue*, not a pitch. For instance, "30 minutes" sends a very different message than "a meeting."

Now, if they are in the mode of wanting to receive a sales pitch, then they're not likely to provide us with the info we are looking for at this stage in the game. But let's learn what we can from them while we are there.

So why not be honest and tell them that the definition isn't complete? Maybe share what the general feedback and requests have been from other parts of the ecosystem?

For instance, "I'm hearing from other members of the ecosystem that they'd like a solution to do x to solve the pain they have associated with y." If this still doesn't do it, you can wrap up any way you want, but this is not wasted time, as you just got great feedback on where this company will sit in your sales pipeline.

So we're trying to learn about the pain to solve, the solution needed, the value proposition, the financial possibilities, the key players, *and* beginning to set up the sales pipeline? Yup, that, too.

When a company like the one we've just discussed teaches you this about themselves, you can put them in the category of "a bit later". They're looking for a baked and solid solution ready to go. It doesn't matter how excited you are about them or their name. It doesn't matter how big they are (remember: the bigger, the slower). Put this in the category of a "nice conversation", and accept it. *Embrace that this is the feedback you got from them.*

There's so much more I could suggest on setup, but you really do need to practice this yourself. This only works for you when you adapt it to your style. If you embrace the idea of *not* selling, and try it a few times, you'll get it.

Question 1 of 2

So now to the first of the two questions, "Does this concept fit with your business priorities?" I've got several items I'm trying to cover with this question.

First, I want this question to facilitate the answer of "no" as easily as possible (if accurate, of course.) So often an audience member feels uncomfortable saying no. Sometimes they don't want to admit they don't quite understand. Sometimes they don't want to do what feels to them like confrontation.

And sometimes they don't want to admit that they don't know ("not knowing" comes up a lot, doesn't it?)

It's important, though, that you get the "no" on the table if it really exists. Otherwise, things drag. And drag. And drag.

Sometimes a "no" means it just doesn't fit. But sometimes when you understand why they said "no", you'll find out that they didn't understand the idea the way you intended. This happens about half the time for me, and I'm able to turn things around and get them on track.

And this is another area where just pushing to sell would do us a tremendous disservice. If we heard "no", we'd be trying to change it to a "yes" instead of objectively identifying why the "no" was happening.

I've done it. But when I'm pushing my agenda it's really hard to be a good listener, and I am far less likely to hear the real reasons for the "no."

Next, by answering the question as stated they will tell you a bit about their priorities-- including the ones that don't apply to our idea.

And this is important. Wow, is this important. This goes back to the idea of me needing to really be empathic and understand all the factors in the other person's world, including other initiatives, politics, firefighting, similar past experiences that didn't go well, and more.

This is where the emotional hot buttons and issues sit a lot of the time, too. Learn what they are, or you will *not* get past them. You can make progress, but you will not get past them to ultimately drive tangible P&L activity.

Lastly on this question, I want the audience member(s) to feel like I really want their input, which, by the way, I honestly do. Most people like to be asked and not told to. Especially the type of decision-makers likely to be your audience members. So that's yet another of many reasons to not sell.

Ask, don't tell. Selling is telling. Don't do that.

Question 2 of 2

Now on to question two, "*If* it does, how can it best serve you?" I didn't it mention before, but don't hold this question until later. Tell them both questions up front. Offering the first word of this question as a hypothetical—"If"—will further your objective of the first question: to send a message that we're not trying to force anything here, and if "no" is the answer, I'm prepared for that.

I have three objectives with this question.

First, I want to hear the *version* of the solution that they need. I'm assuming here that even if I'm on the right track, there is still something I'm missing and need to adjust for. I want to hear that. Really. My experience is that version 1.0 of almost anything exists to tell you what version 2.0 should be, so why not try to short cut that painful first step?

Second, the openness of the question will pull them to tell you about the pain they're trying to solve. We want that too. That's really what this is all about, isn't it? We need to know this. And not from our perspective, but from their perspective. We get that from hearing *them* talk. Not from them agreeing with our interpretation.

Lastly, the word "serve" is important. It hits folks on an emotional level, typically, and that's what I want. I want them to know that I'm there to serve them and not sell. I don't want this to be about me and my company, I want it to be about them.

Creating a tone like this in the conversation will take the relationship to places and levels that otherwise cannot and will not ever happen. This is big. Really big.

So that's it. The silver bullet.

Or two silver bullets if you like. Get a good ecosystem map outlined, get your engagement list together and get on the road with these two questions. The results will open your eyes.

5

Find the Pain

Let's remember, we are engaging the ecosystem for two reasons: to understand what's truly useful and to identify how we can be of service.

This involves learning many things, not the least of which is the pain, or big problem, that needs to be addressed. Let's focus on that, as this is why we're doing whatever it is we're doing with our business.

If you have a "nice conversation", then another, and maybe another, but the relationship is not moving through your sales pipeline then you are not identifying the pain. If you find the pain with your ecosystem and mutually identify and discuss it, companies will immediately ask you to take some action.

And they will sometimes offer to pay you for that. *The lack of this is feedback.* Feedback that you have not found something painful enough for them to pay you, and likely not found something truly valuable.

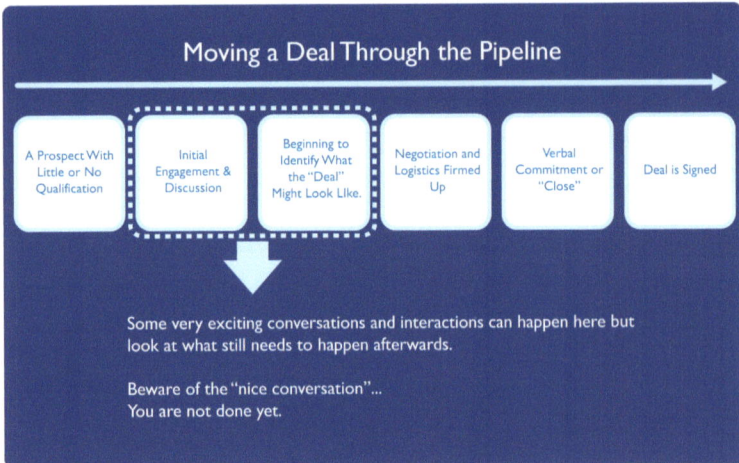

Moving a Deal Through the Pipeline

| A Prospect With Little or No Qualification | Initial Engagement & Discussion | Beginning to Identify What the "Deal" Might Look Like. | Negotiation and Logistics Firmed Up | Verbal Commitment or "Close" | Deal is Signed |

Some very exciting conversations and interactions can happen here but look at what still needs to happen afterwards.

Beware of the "nice conversation"...
You are not done yet.

Ladies and gentlemen, this is why we are here.

We have to find out what is truly useful and how to be of service. That's what sells. What we do and how we do it has to take a back seat to *why* we're doing what we're doing. And this "why" is almost always solving some sort of user experience or business pain. Let's take some time on the concepts of "pain" and "benefits."

Almost everyone I've worked with gets these terms. No one really ever disagrees that they are important concepts and great guides.

But it's rare that they are made the top priority. *Truly* made the top priority. Everyone wants to get to the "how", as that's the tactical, action stuff that let's us get something done.

But I argue that cutting that corner is about as effective as getting in your car, speeding up to 70 mph as fast as possible, and then identifying your destination. Who does that? Stick to the "why?" and many of the decisions you need to make will be much, much easier.

Pain. Not "discomfort", not "nice to have", and not "we'd like."

But *pain.* That is the stuff that typically drives action. Action that results in dedicating resources and buying things. So look for it. Search it out. Find it or maybe your sales will be a "nice to have" also.

Use this as the core of your user story or use case.

This is the beginning, right after you set up a brief user profile or persona. Tell the story of pain from the user's perspective. Solve pain, and you will be doing something very, very useful.

I really learned about identifying pain while holding the post of CEO for an enterprise software startup.

We spent two years experiencing a very typical startup lifecycle. Raise money, spend wisely, get a first customer, prove the technology, try to raise more money, have lots of great conversations with prospective customers and investors, slowly burn through the money, and eventually run out of runway (which means the money ran out.)

The details of the business, the reasons why it went well and could have gone better are irrelevant at this point. What is important is that little phrase I just used: "great conversations."

Little did I know, but I was getting the education of a lifetime. OMG, as our current culture says.

We had absolutely fantastic lead investors, so we were getting introductions and meetings with just about any VC or company that we were interested in. We would put together our pitch, refine it, pitch it, have great conversations, and leave. Sometimes we'd go back for follow up meetings. But at the end of the day we were not selling much.

I knew that I was completely in charge of and the lead for sales and product definition. I know now, though, that even with my willingness, awareness, open-mindedness, and hard work, I could have listened even better-- to the ecosystem as a whole and every member of it.

Among them are a series of experiences that taught and continue to teach me to listen.

Listen to what is said. Listen to what isn't said. Listen to body language. Listen to the statement made by a decision-maker not showing up for a meeting. Listen to what their business is saying is important, whether is has anything to do with my business or not. Listen to long sales cycles.

Find things to listen to. Embrace that they are providing me with answers. In those answers will be the one or two true areas of pain. Or perhaps none at all. Both scenarios are incredibly important to listen for.

There a number of really beneficial reasons to do this. One is that it will act as a grounding force and guide for almost every business decision you make. If it's not addressing this pain, then maybe it should be de-prioritized.

Also, those in engineering or the functions responsible for implementing the "how" need to know this. They need to know why they are doing what they are doing. And by knowing this, they will come up with even better ways of implementing and solving this pain.

I guarantee it.

I've seen it many, many times. If they're simply handed a list of things to go do, you'll rob them, your company, and your customers of this extremely valuable step.

Benefits. Not features. Benefits are what come from the features. This is yet another tough one to stay on track with, but incredibly valuable. Getting this clear will make decisions on features much easier and reduce iterations (and lost development time.)

Think of this as the first step of clarification right after identifying the pain. This is what the customer needs to get from your solution. Again, not what it does or how it does it, but what it delivers for your customers.

I have and will continue to spend very little time in this book discussing technology for a reason. I find that almost no one overlooks it, so I typically go out of my way to make sure that pain, benefits, and the "what" are covered and nailed down. *If I can't define what I need to deliver and what it's supposed to do for my customers, then maybe I shouldn't be building anything yet, right?*

Get fired up about this, as almost every place I've worked for does not embrace and stick to this.

Be different.

I mentioned earlier that I think in slides, so let's use an illustration to outline the engagement process we will walk through to find the pain. We will cover the first four steps from the following illustration now and the final step separately in the next chapter.

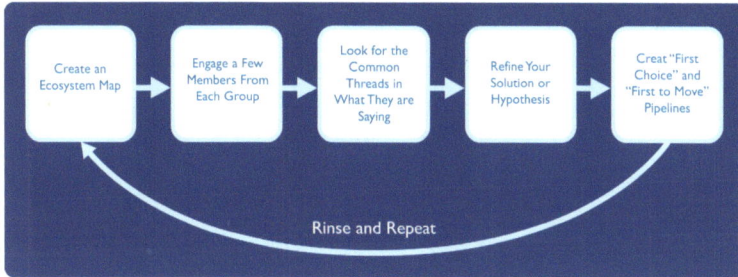

Create an Ecosystem Map → Engage a Few Members From Each Group → Look for the Common Threads in What They are Saying → Refine Your Solution or Hypothesis → Creat "First Choice" and "First to Move" Pipelines

Rinse and Repeat

It's important that you keep this entire process in mind during each step. It will act as a roadmap for you.

If you know what's coming next then you can use that to guide what you are doing now. For instance, if I am engaging a potential partner for the first time to get answers to my two big questions, I know that the specific details of what they say are less important than the common threads they may be tying to from other engagements.

In addition, I know that I'm attempting to experience what it's like to interact, work with, and potentially do business with them. *This holistic view is absolutely critical*.

Create an Ecosystem Map

Some either fear, or hope, that this is a big, detailed, and complicated document. It can't be. If it is, it will likely never get done or it will keep you from getting things done correctly. Keep this simple. Think "3 to 7 categories." Any less than three, and it's not granular enough. Any more than seven, and it will be too complicated.

These categories will be the groups or kinds of ecosystem members that exist or will exist with your offering. Distributors can be a group. Content providers are common. Device manufacturers, designers, or providers of some sort often exist. Sometimes application developers. And don't forget end users, or business users if that is more appropriate.

The way that I usually get to my groupings is to consider the chronological path that the solution takes through the value chain.

For instance, if it's a software solution it may start with a developer. Content necessary and key, or just commodity? Will it be used on a device of some sort that can have some affect on the value chain? Where will it be used? Sometimes the locations of where the solution is used can be a key part of the value chain or value proposition.

In this example it's just four categories. Didn't take much to lay out, and the first version of your map should probably only take minutes to create.

I worked on an indoor positioning solution that used WiFi to locate an individual or device. There were five ecosystem groups on that map. Devices, map data, application developers, venues or locations, and end users.

And don't worry, if it's not perfect, your initial engagements will teach you where your map needs to be updated. This happens to you already, I'm sure. It's those simple little comments that a customer or partner might begin as "You know who you should talk to?..." Or sometimes it's, "I'm not going to take an action on that until you have x on board." So you then go talk to "x." Well, each of those comments are providing you with either good names to put in your categories for engagement, or to create a new category that you might not have had.

The final step is to put three to five names in each of the categories.

There are two reasons for doing this. The first is that you need to create a list of those that you want to go talk to. The second is that by doing this exercise you'll be vetting your map to make sure it's logical.

I've found that I sometimes will identify either redundancy or holes in my map. Sometimes both. The latter is pointed out when I know I have targets I want to talk to, but no category for them.

And resist the urge to list every company you may ever want to talk to. Put them in a spreadsheet somewhere else if you must. Keep this list focused, and call it the "initial engagement target list" if it makes you and others feel better. The goal is to get out of the building and not get dragged into documentation.

Finally, when listing the ecosystem categories and identifying targets to engage, you will likely think of prospects you otherwise would not have thought of.

Make sure this is happening. It's important and evidence of how this exercise should be pulling you out of the box. It's not meant to be a routine exercise. It's a valuable and important step that many overlook by simply going after the big or familiar names and, therefore, missing the others.

If you start by putting your current targets on this new map by themselves, you'll likely see a bias you currently have towards certain ecosystem areas. This visual can be priceless.

Engage a Few Members From Each Ecosystem Group

So it's time to start putting this into action. You've got your map. You've got your list of targets. Now get out of the building.

Let's set the stage here, though, for having some patience. Not a lot, but a little. (And sometimes a little can feel like infinitely more than none, can't it? But do it, please.) It's important to not try to "figure out" the whole thing after each meeting. I've done it, and I've been with others that have done it.

It's that walk to the car after leaving the building where you look at each other and go, "So it looks like they want [fill in the blank], and we should do [fill in the other blank] to make this work."

Nope. That's just one data point, folks. It might end up being true, but our goal here is to understand what the *ecosystem* wants, not that one member (no matter how great they might be.)

I've found, by the way, that when someone big wants something, they can be easily and willingly taught to change course when I bring them *real* data to the contrary from the rest of the ecosystem. In fact, this is common.

This is one of the benefits of engaging across the entire ecosystem to get a holistic view and knowledge base of factual data. Sharing "what the rest of the ecosystem is saying" is a great way to be of service and build relationships. A very great way.

So start meeting.

Use the two questions and simple setup described in the previous chapter. Take notes, but fight the urge to set any of your notes in stone, as each meeting will begin to point out the true learnings of the previous.

You see, this is really where the patience comes in. What I need to learn is not typically revealed to me in the beginning. It's the holistic view of all of my engagements that gives me true direction.

Now here's a suggestion that you might see coming, or you might not, but either way it will rock the boat.

Do not use slides.

Now hold on for a minute. That may sound crazy to some of you.

I actually really like PowerPoint. In fact, this book is one of the longest word processing documents I've ever written, as I almost always organize my message with slides. Someone once told me that I "think in PowerPoint."

As cute as that is, it's really quite accurate. I'm very visual. I like to tell stories in 5-10 slides. The process of creating those slides is very helpful to me. It forces me to weed out the fluff and get to the point.

So why no slides?

Simple. When I use slides I talk. Not my audience members.

And when I talk, I don't learn anything. When they talk, I learn.

I once engaged an entire ecosystem across, five categories of partners, from the bottom of the IT stack to the top, including sixty companies, tens of thousands of airline miles, and I don't remember using any slides. Yes, it surprised me when I looked back at it, too.

But it happened without slides. And it's probably one of the best projects I ever executed. And they were by far the most efficient engagements I've ever had.

Embrace *Do not use slides*, and it's a game-changer.

Looking For The Common Threads

So we've started our meetings with ecosystem members.

We're getting some good insight. We're being patient during and after each meeting for the first six or seven meetings. Now, what are the common threads in what we've been hearing? Are there one or two real points of pain that they want addressed? Is there an ecosystem member or category that keeps getting mentioned?

Plan to do this inventory every five meetings or so. Not less, not more.

There is likely something beginning to stand out. Grab that and either lock in part of the hypothesis you had, or modify it if appropriate.

From here on out we're going to test this common thread in each of our other engagements. But it's not usually until I've engaged at least a half dozen ecosystem members that I can do this. And it's usually closer to a full dozen, so don't be tempted to cut corners here.

And there don't have to be a lot of common threads. Usually just one or two. Many times they relate to the use case that needs to be solved for. Not so much technologies. Not so much the details of the solution. Usually they relate to priorities and pain.

Now be sure to share these common threads during future meetings, too. Not only will they act as catalysts for discussion, but by sharing them you'll be testing a hypothesis.

The feedback will tell you how much of a common thread it really is or isn't. A phrase I use a lot is, "What I'm hearing from the ecosystem is that they're top priority is to create a solution that addresses [pain description inserted here]."

Refine Your Solution or Hypothesis

So if you've been open to implementing the steps put forth here, and modified and adjusted as you went along, you likely have a couple of big learnings under your belt. *Don't look for a laundry list here.* Let the one or two big themes guide you.

By this time, the ecosystem has told you what they want. Just write it down. Do a one-to-two page use case, or story. But don't be tricked into writing down the "how". You need to focus on the "what."

This means, bluntly, leave out the technology.

Leave out data sheet features. Leave out specifications. Those are all too detailed and will pull you away from the clearly specifying the *pain* that needs to be solved for and the *benefits* that have to be delivered.

You can - and will without even trying - get to all those fun specs later.

A Thought on "Rinse and Repeat"

You are going to iterate through this whole process. You can plan for it, or you can experience the pain and inefficiency of not planning for it. You will iterate either way.

I mentioned beginning to look for common threads after about ten or so engagements.

My experience is that my learning "inflection points" happen every ten or so engagements. This does not take long if you are getting outside the building, so don't tell yourself that this is a long time to wait. I mentioned earlier how I engaged sixty companies in forty-five days. That is not a long time.

This mindset is important not just to plan for iterations, but also to have in your mind an acceptance that you don't have to get it perfect at every step. You get a chance to completely reverse your assumptions if you need to.

Get the steps clear in your mind. I tend to think of them very simply as: three-to-seven categories, target list, big themes, and my two pipelines (which I will talk about in the next chapter.) And sometimes I even shorten it to big themes and two pipelines. You can come up with your own approach, but do get one. It'll help to keep things simple and keep you on track.

As a reminder, *do not get hung up on mechanics of this process*. The steps are important guides to follow, but our primary goal with them is to create an atmosphere that allows us to hear the answers we need to hear - the answers to those two important questions we use for all of our engagements.

And they are not always the answers we expect.

In fact, many, many times they are not what we expect at all. Be very open to the answers and guides that are being handed to you as you move through your engagements. Believe me, they are being handed to you if you are listening. Really listening. This is what it takes to identify what is truly useful and how to be of service.

6

Two Pipelines are Better Than One

Now it is time to identify and outline the two pipelines that our ecosystem engagement has given us. Yes, I said *two* pipelines.

We've met a lot of companies by this time. And we have our favorites for who we'd like to work with first. In the early stages of my career these companies would have been the big, marquee names. The market leaders. Those that would drive the big volumes. I now call these the "First Choice" companies.

The more I've been responsible for starting businesses or growing in new areas, though, my favorites are small or medium sized companies. Almost never those big, popular companies that my friends and family have heard of. Almost never what the top executives in my company want to hear about.

The reason I like them, though, is simple: *their sense of urgency to execute.*

I call these the "First to Move" companies. The big guys, or those leading markets, have less pain. They're not foolish, though. They have excellent strategies, and they'll act on them. But almost by definition, they have less pain, will take longer to make decisions, and take longer to get things into action and my revenue stream going.

The First to Move firms are typically lagging or sometimes just new to the party. Their "pain" is that they are somehow behind or need to validate their spot in the ecosystem. They'll take action, and I want that, so they become my favorites to *start* with.

I've been able to meet and get to know a bunch of companies throughout my career. And not just their businesses, but their priorities and the *people*. That's important. The *people*. My experience is that the correlation between "great to work with" people and great P&L success is quite high.

So I weight this very heavily. This can be tough sometimes, though, as there are high emotions around the marquee names. But "great to work with" means to me that they will actually work. They will put things into action. And I and my company won't have to do much to get that done. And we won't have to wait too long. So isn't that a great way to start? Keep this in mind when identifying your First to Move companies.

So do it. Create these two lists. One that has the three to five firms that you think would fill out a great ecosystem in the short term and the three to five firms that would make the blockbuster ecosystem later.

Now work both pipelines in parallel. You will have names in the latter category that you will not want there. Too bad. Deal with it. They are there for a reason. You talked to them. You heard about them from other ecosystem members. Your gut is right. They will not move fast enough.

Remember one of the key learnings that a lead investor shared with me? "It takes 18 months to do a deal with a big company."

He's right.

Keep both pipelines in mind moving forward, driving your First to Move folks into action as fast as possible and fostering the First Choice group at whatever pace they will accept.

Leading Your Organization to Accept "First to Move"

It is important to think this through a bit and even formulate a strategy if necessary. Your organization might need some help to accept and embrace the concept of a "First to Move" pipeline. As we mentioned earlier, there is natural excitement and focus on "First Choice" that can be hard to avoid or overcome.

So leave the building and get answers. In fact, be verbal about that, and announce your engagement intentions. Let the appropriate parties know of your engagement plan. Show them your list of targets. You might need to do this tactfully, though, as some of your ecosystem categories or groups might not be intuitive targets to your organization.

Almost always my organizations want to target only the First Choice folks. Why wouldn't they? They're "first." But as we discussed earlier, we know we'll have some first movers that won't be in this group, and we need to engage them, too.

Perhaps we will have even more of them and we will see them more often. But I typically don't announce this. I just do it, with occasional updates on interesting learnings or progress. I do this only occasionally, so that folks don't get the idea that it's all that I'm doing and that I'm abandoning their first choices.

And when I do mention these engagements I tend to mention them a bit further down in my updates, perhaps after a note on a first choice engagement. But do mention the first to move group, as you want to plant seeds for what are likely going to be the first partners and customers that everyone works with.

It's very important to do this, so find a balance in how you communicate your activities. This First to Move group should not be hidden. It's always met with positive responses, as long as folks think you've still got the First Choice targets solidly on your list.

A final important note on notifying folks of your engagement plan relates to setting expectations.

If there is some sort of "plan" to engage out there and communicated to your organization, it must mean that we're not done yet. This is important, because we need to remember that we do not have all the answers, right?

And if folks understand the scope of the plan (for example, 30 companies in 45 days) they'll understand that any reports on the initial engagements are just that —initial. Also, by formalizing the process of engaging outside parties, it becomes visible to executives and leaders. This also makes it a deliverable, which generates momentum to make sure it's completed without you having to push for it.

7

Do Something Real ASAP

By this time you've engaged a lot of companies, identified the top pain points to address, outlined two pipelines, and have ready to go several partners and customers that you want to work with.

That's really good, but we have to get something into action, as well as see and feel something tangible soon. This is important for you, your company and teammates, and most importantly the P&L.

This doesn't require a big project plan or set of vision slides. It just means you need to do something tangible. Something that folks both internal and external can look at and that allows them to experience progress. But be patient and careful in how you set it up internally. Much like your work in leading an organization through embracing two pipelines, the set up is key: many times stakeholders will see the benefit of your tangible progress only *after* it is in place. *The discussion of it beforehand many times is just a discussion, so discuss sparingly.*

79

I believe that most, if not all, business efforts are iterations. You can plan for this or not plan for this. Either way you are going to iterate. Planning for it, however, is far less painful. With this in mind, choose something small, easily completed, and with a short lead-time. I call these "bite-sized chunks." The work you've done with your "First to Move" pipeline has probably already defined this for you.

There are likely multiple demos, alpha tests, or trials that will fit the bill perfectly. This list, cross-checked with the priorities of your favorite partners or customers, should identify the first bite-sized chunk to get done.

Getting something into action means you can vet your pipelines. By attempting to get something like a demo, trial, or the like into place, you will understand just how serious your customers and partners are. There is no substitute for asking someone to pay for something or dedicate resources. This is where the rubber meets the road.

There are also huge benefits to getting your solution drafted or prototyped for testing. Even the best ecosystem members will not get it perfect at first. So the sooner you get something real into the hands of customers, the sooner you can iterate to the real winner.

And let's not forget that the devil is in the details. This is always true. The definition of a solution can appear complete, but until you need to build it or deliver it, you likely have not thought through all of the pieces necessary.

It's likely that you can deliver all that you need to, but you want to find out as fast as possible what you might have overlooked. Get things into action, and you'll find out fast.

Finally, you will more effectively lead others by taking action. Words, slides, and other material will influence and capture attention. But true, sustainable momentum will be created by tangible progress. Part of this is tactical, but much of it is emotional. Once something is really being built, or worked on with customers, it grows roots. It moves from "if" and "should we?" to "it is due" and "we are". *Do not underestimate this.* It's one powerful tool.

I think you get the point. Listen to what your ecosystem has asked for. Define simply and small. Get it done fast. The momentum you generate for your employer and others in the ecosystem will be exciting and of tremendous service. Remember: You can plan to iterate or not, but either way you are going to iterate. Start now.

Conclusion

So: there you have it.

List your questions inside the building, but do not try to answer them there.

Get out as soon as you can. Keep it simple. Don't wait to have the perfect story. Create a quick ecosystem map and have comfortable conversations with three folks in each category. Be sure not to pitch or sell.

 Just talk to them and be a really, really good listener.

How do you talk to them? Simply state verbally your idea and ask them if it aligns with their business priorities, and if it does, how it can best serve them.

That is it. Don't say more until they've answered these two questions. Listen. Fight the urge to do more. The answers to these two simple questions will both educate you and tell you what to ask about and discuss next. I promise.

Focus on people and what is important to them and their business. Not networking, but *people*. Do not focus on yourself and your agenda. Find out how you can best serve them. Identify what you have in common and how those synergies might lead to working together. If there are no synergies, accept this outcome and be at peace with it.

Ask for and offer introductions to other like-minded folks.

It's about people. If you understand and embrace this, things will be a lot easier.

Be very honest about the real status of your engagements.

Is it a "First Choice" firm that would be awesome to have on board, but will likely take one to two years to get into action? Or is it a "First to Move" firm that, while less exciting to my company, will be very good to work with, quick to move, and a fantastic start to my ecosystem.

Again, be honest about this. You will not change which group they are really in, so having a good handle on the truth and what is being told to you will allow you to do something useful and be of service much faster.

And get it all into action. Everyone, including you, needs to see this. You will feel better and you will learn more by beginning to build something as soon as your ecosystem has made it clear what it wants.

Finally, please be okay with not knowing the answers.

The reality is that you and I typically don't know, so let's be honest about it and get the best answers as fast a possible. This is the key. I started the book with this concept for a reason. It is the fundamental shift in thinking that I have had to make to implement what I've outlined for you.

There are no half measures here. You must embrace this.

If you truly embrace it you will not feel like you are admitting defeat, as most feel immediately empowered and energized. It's the key.

It's also quite counter-intuitive… but that's why I wrote this book.

I hope *The Answers Are Outside The Building* has been helpful to you. As I stated in the beginning, my mission is to do truly useful things and to be of service. I appreciate the opportunity to have (hopefully) done that for you here.

I think the title really says it all. Get out of the building to get your answers. Just do it. Don't wait any longer to try what's been laid out for you in this book.

I wish I'd known these things much earlier in my career. Make it part of your development plans for those you manage and lead. I have. The folks on my teams usually appreciate it, as "getting outside" liberates them to get real answers that they knew they didn't have and let's them be honest about it.

I wish you well in using some or all of what I've presented here.

One last thing: please let me know if I can be of service to you in any way.

Stu Heilsberg | San Diego | March 2013

Credits

Edited by Brendan Howley

Illustrations by Julie Kuang

Acknowledgements

This book is about people more than it is about business process, so it's natural that there are a number of folks I'd like to recognize here.

I'd like to thank those below and those I might be overlooking. You have all been fantastic teammates, mentors, and friends.

--Thank you!

My teammates at Qualcomm, including but not limited to: Joan Waltman, Tom Doyle, Will Ater, Greg Rothnem, Nashina Asaria, David Wood, Scott Yankton, Joe Rassenti, and Craig Lauer. We did some great work together, and I appreciated greatly the opportunity to exercise and refine much of what is in this book with you. I look forward to working with all of you again soon.

To Steve Campbell, Bob Packer, and Craig Elliott, lead investors at the startup I led, for your leadership, mentorship, and friendship.

Dave Derby, former CEO and board member of several companies. Most importantly, Dave has been a friend, mentor, and almost a spiritual advisor, the value of which cannot be measured.

To my new found friends and media experts Brendan Howley and Gunther Sonnenfeld. For sharing your experience and your ongoing guidance. What a great connection we've made.

And last but not least my wife, Dina. Thank you for your unending support, friendship, companionship, and awesomeness. I love you.

###

Connect with me online at:

http://www.linkedin.com/in/stuheilsberg/

https://twitter.com/sheilsberg

http://www.heilsbergconsulting.com/

stuh@alum.mit.edu

Participate in my blog at:

http://stuheilsberg.wordpress.com

About the Author

The Beginning

Originally from Long Island and having grown up mostly in Florida, I headed off to college far from home and attended MIT. I was an average student there, graduated with my Bachelor's Degree in Mechanical Engineering, and went on to work at Motorola as an engineer right after college.

I worked mostly on what we called two-way radios, but what I typically describe as "the walkie-talkies that the police use." It was a fantastic experience, providing me with the opportunity to learn from some great folks and get exposure to everything from plastics, to sheet metal, to castings, to rubber molded parts, and more. A really great way to start my career, and I am appreciative for that opportunity. To this day, it's one of my favorite teams.

I expected, even as an undergraduate, to leave engineering after a few years. I did so, and went immediately into Product Management at Motorola, where I was on a team that managed many, many mobile phones sold in the U.S. Another great experience that began to expose me to the benefits of focusing on end users and allowing their needs to pull products into the right definitions.

Many ask about the difficulties of making this transition from the technical side to the business side. It was not difficult for me and was a very natural process, where I ramped up very quickly. I had for many years stated that I wanted to learn how to run a business, so that was likely a good indicator that this shift would be a good fit for me.

Next came my MBA at Kellogg in Chicago. A great program that I completed while working full time at Motorola. I began to pick up some really great tools and insights, having had a couple of years of work experience under my belt. Among these tools was the concept of Segmentation, Targeting, and Positioning. Little did I know that it was one of many early stage seeds being planted in my head telling me to focus outside first, inside second.

I finished my MBA and immediately joined an enterprise hardware company in San Diego, filling a Senior Product Manager role for two years. Nothing big to report on this, except that I really started to identify that I liked consumer-focused solutions. They provided me with the outside-in pull that I gravitated towards.

I said in those days that consumer solutions tended to be easier, because if you got it wrong, you immediately got feedback. It might be lack of sales or support calls, but somehow you got that feedback directly.

With this growing realization I began to search for a more consumer-focused company, and wow did I find one.

Intuit.

Among the bright spots in my career is most assuredly this job. I was hired on as the head of Product Management for the TurboTax product line. I had a great team handed to me to lead, and I was part of a fantastic business unit.

I spent four years in that post, where revenues grew, as did profitability. It was a culture that not only focused on end users first, but asked the question "How can we 'wow' the customer?"

Absolutely fantastic. And I attribute this to the founder, Scott Cook. Even a decade after starting the company, his style was prevalent. Likely, due to his regular involvement at all levels in a very helpful and functional way.

The Real Beginning

I left Intuit and began what I think is the real journey to understanding what it takes to engage an ecosystem. This a bit humbling to admit, but I think incredibly important to put on the table.

Think about it. I was in my mid-thirties and had led product lines well into the hundreds of millions of dollars, but to be perfectly honest, much of what I needed was handed to me by my company. This isn't bad, but it's a reality for many individuals, and is better recognized than not.

I received a call from a former colleague at Intuit asking me to meet to discuss his startup. He had been working on new approach for database integration and lined up some lead investors, but those investors wanted him to have a business leader. To make a long story short, we met, discussed, worked on it a bit together, and I accepted the position of CEO about a month later.

We then spent two years experiencing a very typical startup lifecycle, as I mentioned in the body of the book.

Little did I know, but I was getting the education of a lifetime. The blessing was that I was unconsciously beginning to exercise and embrace "getting out of the building" and… didn't know it.

My Focus on Business Development

So there I was. Ex-CEO of a startup. I've just had the best experience ever, and I'm looking for my next gig. I took a little time off, but began to look for posts in other small companies.

A very good friend suggested I check out a business development spot at Qualcomm, but I immediately shunned it, as that was the big company in our hometown of San Diego, and far too large, slow, bureaucratic, etc.

Long story short, I ended up interviewing, loved the people in the division I was introduced to, and hoped they'd hire me. Funny, huh? They did hire me, and so began an incredible four-year experience.

As outlined in the first chapter of this book, I had the opportunity to work on three projects during this time. Each required me and my teammates to get outside of the building, get the answers, and identify the best way for Qualcomm to aim itself.

We gathered feedback from all over the ecosystem and the world. We put it together, defined a roadmap that was consistent with the needs of the market and the business priorities of the ecosystem.

We used all of the relationships we had built from those engagements to prioritize a sales and partner pipeline. Then we put things into action.

It was easier each time I did it. Something was working really, really well.

Each project was green-lighted, where one even became it's own division.

And so began what I'm going to call an awakening in my career and in me. A realization of a process that I hadn't been taught directly, nor had I intended to create. But one that worked really well.

There have been a number of posts in my career since those businesses at Qualcomm, but the story seems to always revolve around this approach of getting my engagement list outlined and going outside to learn and get to the answers.

This is my passion.

As of the date of this book's publishing, my activities center on management consulting for companies of all sizes. Much of my work is in mobile, including apps, devices, services, and payments.

I have a relentless focus now on executing the principles of this book.

I work with others constantly to get answers outside of the building.

I don't want to sell, but I love it when my efforts result in sales.

I'm constantly looking to connect with great people.

And my mission is to find opportunities where I can do truly useful things and be of service.

www.ingramcontent.com/pod-product-compliance
Lightning Source LLC
Chambersburg PA
CBHW041311210326
41599CB00003B/73